D0848570

Spotlight on
Kids Can Code

Understanding Coding by Building

ALGORITHMS

Patricia Harris

PowerKiDS press

New York

Published in 2017 by The Rosen Publishing Group, Inc.
29 East 21st Street, New York, NY 10010

First Edition

Editor: Greg Roza
Book Design: Michael J. Flynn

Photo Credits: Cover Blend Images - KidStock/Brand X Pictures/Getty Images; cover, pp. 1, 3–24 (coding background) Lukas Rs/Shutterstock.com; p. 5 Eduard Kim/Shutterstock.com; p. 6 https://commons.wikimedia.org/wiki/File:Alan_Turing_Aged_16.jpg; p. 7 Carl Mydans/The LIFE Picture Collection/Getty Images; p. 8 S-F/Shutterstock.com; p. 9 https://commons.wikimedia.org/wiki/File:Turing_Machine_Model_Davey_detail_2012.jpg; p. 11 Morrowind/Shutterstock.com; p. 13 https://commons.wikimedia.org/wiki/File:PR2_robot_reads_the_Mythical_Man-Month.jpg#/media/File:PR2_robot_reads_the_Mythical_Man-Month.jpg; p. 15 Shyamalamuralinath/Shutterstock.com; p. 19 FabrikaSimf/Shutterstock.com; p. 21 espies/Shutterstock.com.

Cataloging-in-Publication Data

Names: Harris, Patricia.
Title: Understanding coding by building algorithms / Patricia Harris.
Description: New York : PowerKids Press, 2017. | Series: Spotlight on kids can code| Includes index.
Identifiers: ISBN 9781499427936 (pbk.) | ISBN 9781499428230 (library bound) | ISBN 9781499429541 (6 pack)
Subjects: LCSH: Computer programming–Juvenile literature. | Programming languages (Electronic computers)–Juvenile literature. | Computers–Juvenile literature.
Classification: LCC QA76.52 H37 2017 | DDC 005–dc23

Manufactured in the United States of America

CPSIA Compliance Information: Batch #BW17PK: For Further Information contact Rosen Publishing, New York, New York at 1-800-237-9932

Contents

Ancient Origins

In computer science and math, an algorithm is a set of steps to be followed to accomplish a task. Algorithms must have an end, or a task to complete. The steps may be followed by a person or a computer. Whoever or whatever is following the instructions must have the information and skills needed to do the steps.

The term "algorithm" is linked to the name Muḥammad ibn Mūsā al-Khwārizmī (c. 780–c. 850). He was a Muslim scholar who introduced new ideas into mathematics. He lived in the region now known as the Middle East and may have been born in one of the areas known today as Iraq or Uzbekistan. He applied a step-by-step approach to solving math problems and wrote about solving equations.

The words **"algebra"** and "algorithm" come from al-Khwārizmī's name. His name was often spelled "Algoritmi" by Europeans.

Abstract Thinking

During the 1930s, English computer scientist Alan Turing expanded the idea of step-by-step instructions in his Turing machine. The Turing machine is not a machine that you can see. It's an **abstract** machine. The Turing machine uses algorithms to solve problems. The machine follows instructions to complete a simple mechanical operation. Then it goes to the next step or stops working. It always completes the steps in the order they are given.

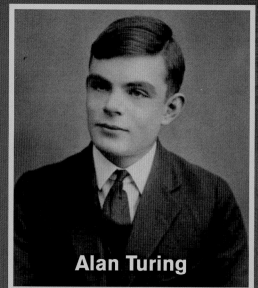

Alan Turing

Breaking the Code

The Turing machine can **simulate** any algorithm. The machine has an **infinitely** long tape of squares or cells. This acts as the computer's memory. The machine has an "eye" that can read one square at a time. The machine follows the instruction and then moves on to a new square to follow the next instruction. Turing showed that a machine could be made to calculate the answer to any mathematical problem, no matter how **complex** it is.

Early computers used tape or punch cards for **input** and **output** (I/O). Today's computers use digital memory that allows data to be read or written anywhere on the storage device.

Computer scientists today need more than a Turing machine to solve problems. Turing machines are important when thinking about coding, but they were designed to provide mechanical output in the form of a tape. Computer scientists know that for solving modern problems they need more than mechanical output.

The thinking behind a Turing machine is similar to the thought processes used for computer programming today. Programmers use a step-by-step approach to solving problems. Before they write code, programmers must think of all the steps the computer will need to perform and the order those steps need to be in. They think about the data for their algorithms and ask themselves: What inputs are needed and what outputs can be produced?

Coders think of ways to break a complex task into smaller steps that can be placed in algorithms. They think about how they will store the output when each algorithm runs. That also means they must consider how sets of steps will be arranged. Algorithms involve a lot of thinking, but they help make coding more **efficient**.

I'm really glad I can do the little steps!

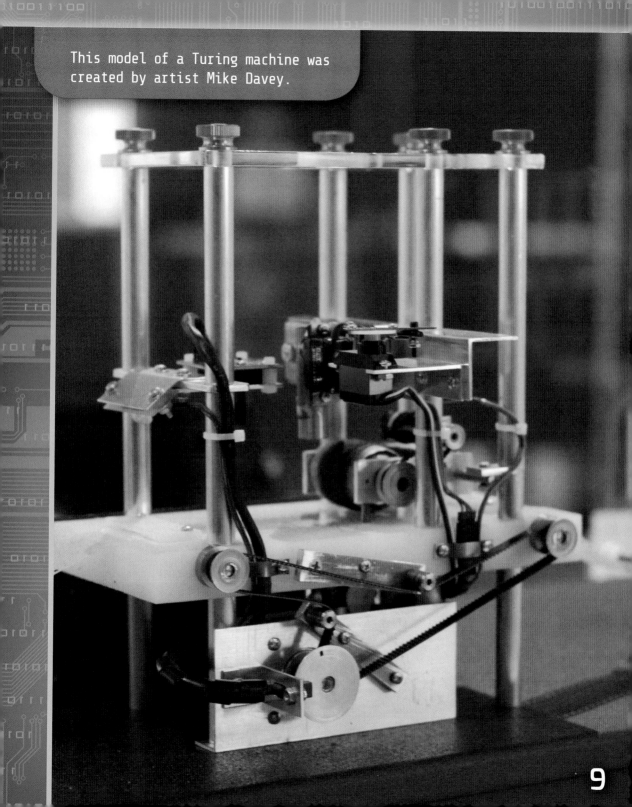

This model of a Turing machine was created by artist Mike Davey.

Turing Complete

Today, some programming languages are said to be "Turing complete." That means the language can ask the computer to do all the algorithms that can be accomplished by a Turing machine. In the real world, the tasks are limited by time, the power of the computer, and the ability of a person to work with complex data.

Software allows programmers to think about a few operations at a time. Programmers only have to work with some of the algorithms needed to complete a task. The software handles much of the work the computer needs to do. This means programmers don't repeat a lot of work in every program, and they don't have to work with all the data needed to complete a task.

There are numerous algorithms used for different purposes. Good coders understand the different kinds, such as the quicksort algorithm and the divide-and-conquer algorithm. Some algorithms are named after the mathematicians who first recorded them.

Using Algorithms

Programming a computer to control a robot would be a big job if every programmer had to start from the beginning. To avoid this, computer programmers use abstraction, which means they work with a small part of the problem. For example, they may be asked to write code to move the robot's arm to a specific position rather than coding all the robot's movements.

Using or developing algorithms to solve problems is really what programming is all about. Programmers need to know about common algorithms and understand what's happening when an algorithm is run. They also need to understand why certain algorithms are written the way they are. Even when working on a small part of a task, programmers must be able to put together all they know about algorithms.

Breaking the Code

In 2015, Mehrnoosh Sadrzadeh wrote an article titled "How to Feed and Raise a Wikipedia Robo-Editor." This article talks about how to use **artificial intelligence** (AI) algorithms to edit texts. Sadrzadeh made the point that AI algorithms can spot fake reviews on Wikipedia 90 percent of the time. Of course, the computer has to have good data input!

The PR2, shown here, is a programmable robot. This one has been programmed to read.

Flowcharts and Pseudocode

Programmers use flowcharts and pseudocode to show the way an algorithm will be written. To describe any algorithm, they may use both methods or just one. A flowchart is a diagram that uses special symbols to show the steps in an algorithm. Pseudocode is a way to describe an algorithm using English or special symbols.

Flowcharts have standard symbols, but pseudocode does not. While pseudocode is not true code, programmers may use items that look a lot like code instead of using plain English. In pseudocode, you show how the algorithm for each part of the code will function and then break each algorithm into **modules** that can interact with and communicate with other modules. A simple algorithm can have just a few steps and may have no modules.

When first starting to write new code, the coder can write pseudocode and then develop a flowchart to show the steps needed.

Flowchart

Start

Input hours

Input rate

pay = hours * rate

Stop

Pseudocode

```
BEGIN
    input hours
    input rate
    pay = hours * rate
    print pay
END
```

Let's Get Flowing

Flowcharts have six basic symbols, although many others can be used. A terminal is a rectangle with rounded corners. It means start or stop depending on where it appears. A parallelogram shows input and output (I/O). A rectangle shows processes or actions. This symbol can be used to tell the value of a **variable** when it's first used in a program. It can also tell what happens to the input.

Arrows show the flow of actions. Decisions are shown with a diamond. They have two exit points—one for true or "yes" and one for false or "no." Decisions need arrows that show what happens for a "yes" answer and a "no" answer. A connector circle is used to represent a break in the flow.

Here is the flowchart for an algorithm for logging into Gmail. This chart summarizes three steps. Step one is to go to the Gmail page. Step two is to enter the ID information. Step three is to check if the information is correct and take the right action.

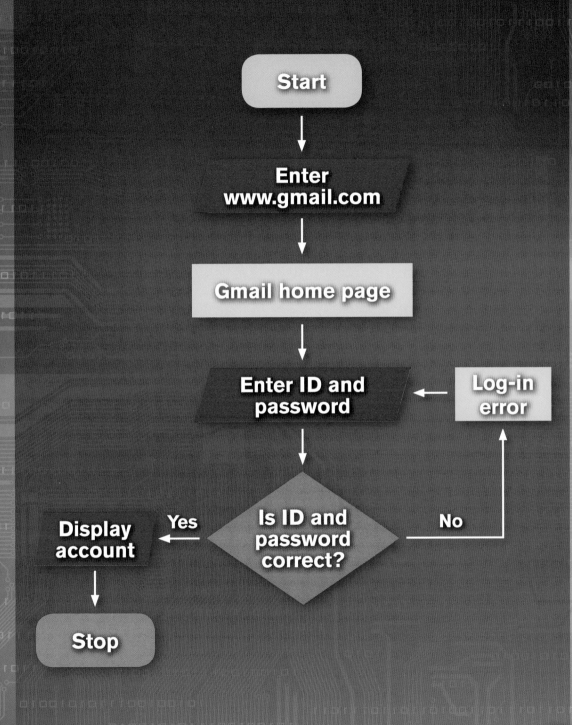

Let's make a flowchart and write pseudocode for a simple math task. Before you do this for any algorithm, however, it helps to write the algorithm in English. The algorithm for adding two numbers is expressed in the following way: Set the sum to 0, enter the numbers, add them, store as sum (making the sum equal to a new number), and print sum. Here is the flowchart for that statement when the two numbers are 5 and 6.

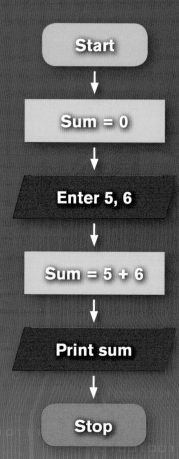

Here is the psuedocode for the same task. This pseudocode looks a little like coding in a programming language and a lot less like plain English!

```
Descriptive information
/*x and y will store the input and sum will store the result
*/
code starts here:
SumOf2Numbers()
Begin
    Read: x,y;
    Set sum = x+y;
    Print:sum;
End
```

You can use a word processor to write pseudocode on a computer.

Try It Yourself

You have learned a lot about algorithms and flowcharts. You can put together what you have learned by writing an algorithm for adding three numbers.

Here is a statement for this algorithm in English that tells the steps of the process:

1. Set the sum = 0 and count = 0.
2. Enter n (which stands for number).
3. Find the sum + n, set it to sum, and increase the count by 1.
4. If count = 3 is no, go to step 2; if yes, print sum.

Some hints will help you get started:

1. The first step is a process.
2. You will need an I/O box.
3. You will need to use a decision point to know when to stop and print out the sum.

Need more help? Check out the finished flowchart on page 22.

21

Solution to Adding Three Numbers

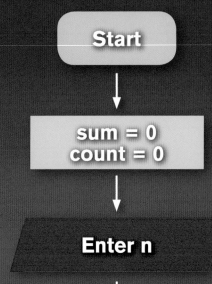

Start

sum = 0
count = 0

Enter n

sum = sum + n
count = count + 1

Is count = 3?

Print sum   Yes   No

Stop

Glossary

abstract: A thought or idea rather than a physical object.

algebra: A kind of math that involves letters representing number variables.

artificial intelligence: An area of computer science that deals with giving machines the ability to think like people.

complex: Having many parts.

efficient: Capable of producing desired results without wasting materials, time, or energy.

infinitely: Without limits; endless.

input: Information entered into a computer.

module: A part of a computer or computer program that does a particular job.

output: The answers received from a computer.

simulate: To represent the operation of a process by means of another system, such as a computer.

software: Programs that run on computers and perform certain functions.

variable: In mathematics, a quantity that may change when other conditions change.

Index

Websites

Due to the changing nature of Internet links, PowerKids Press has developed an online list of websites related to the subject of this book. This site is updated regularly. Please use this link to access the list: www.powerkidslinks.com/kcc/algo